HOW IT ALL BEGAN

AN OVERVIEW OF GENESIS

JACK HAYFORD
SCOTT BAUER • JACK HAMILTON

HOW IT ALL BEGAN
A Practical, Introductory Guidebook For A Comprehensive Overview in the Bible Book of GENESIS

Copyright © 1996 Living Way Ministries.

Unless otherwise noted, all Scripture references are from the New King James Version:
Copyright © 1979, 1980, 1982 by Thomas Nelson, Inc., Nashville, Tennessee.
Maps and illustrations taken from the *Nelson's Complete Book of Bible Maps and Charts*, ©1993, Thomas Nelson, Inc. Used by permission.
Outline of Genesis taken from the *Spirit-Filled Life Bible*, ©1991, Thomas Nelson, Inc. Used by permission.

Photograph of Dr. Jack Hayford by Harry Langdon, Jr.
Photographs of Dr. Scott Bauer and Dr. Jack Hamilton by Christopher Glenn Photography.

Published by Living Way Ministries
14300 Sherman Way
Van Nuys, CA (USA) 91405-2499
(818) 779-8400 • (800) 776-8180

ISBN 0-916847-18-7
Printed in the United States of America

TABLE OF CONTENTS

GROWING WITH THE BIBLE BOOK-A-MONTH STUDIES

Disciples of the Lord Jesus Christ know it: *There is no substitute for the Word of God in our daily lives!* Still, many find that the formation of a satisfying, fulfilling discipline in reading and studying God's Word is not easy. In contrast, many fall into a merely regimented or legalistic habit that eventually withers for lack of the Holy Spirit's breath upon it. Others have difficulty finding direction or maintaining focus; besides, we all need help to keep us moving forward *through* the Word.

The formulation of the "Bible Book-A-Month" concept was born in the heart of Dr. Jack Hayford, who, as a pastor, constantly seeks improved means of helping people achieve three things: *systematic, substantial,* and *thorough* coverage of the Bible. Each is important to accomplish the objective of good Bible study, and they can be realized through this plan.

(1) It's <u>systematic</u>, by reason of the *month-by-month* advancement of the program; (2) it's <u>substantial</u>, because of the *spiritual weight* of the triangular

approach of study employed; and (3) it's <u>thorough</u>, for *every book* of the Bible is incorporated in it.

THE TRIANGULAR APPROACH

There are many worthwhile approaches to a study of the Holy Bible. For example, "synthetic" study—which draws together highlights to provide a quick grasp of a book; "critical" study—which assesses the ancient textual resources that authenticate the trustworthiness of the book as a document; or "verse-by-verse" study—which seeks to exhaust every book of the totality of its content.

Distinct from any of these, the "Bible Book-A-Month" study seeks to achieve the maximum possible grasp of a book's truth while keeping a pace forward which sustains the average Bible student's interest. It is <u>demanding</u> enough in its *academics* to seriously engage those interested in intelligent, thought-provoking study. Yet it is <u>dynamic</u> enough in its *movement* to avoid losing passion, and to keep each student at a point of continuous anticipation. This is done through use of a **"triangular approach"** to each book—which focuses the three primary things to be found in every book of the Bible.

1. Each Bible book contains an *essential message*: the core concepts which distinguish that book and provide its place in God's Word. This is found in *towering truths* and *pillar passages* within that book. These together provide a rich overview of the Holy Spirit's theme and thrust in that book of the Bible.

2. Each Bible book presents *problems* and evokes *questions* rising from the need to integrate that book's content with the whole Bible, as well as to interpret its content as it addresses current issues. Good Bible study helps questioners find *satisfactory answers* to reasoned inquiry, even as it demonstrates the *relevancy* of God's Word to today's social problems. Thus, we discover the power of the Holy Spirit—present to reveal Christ to the world—TODAY!

3. Each Bible book provides *practical wisdom* and *personal guidance*; it sheds light on the believer's daily walk and service as he or she follows Jesus Christ. Healthy study in God's Word should provide *information* and *inspiration*, but only as it issues in *incarnation* does it achieve its goal! In each book, *insights for faithful, fruitful pathways* will show how to adopt, adapt, and apply the Bible to your life, as Jesus' disciple.

These perspectives provide the viewpoints which "triangulate" on the text: each book studied through three lessons which unfold the truth of God's Word noting one of the above three values. The "Bible Book-A-Month" triangular approach works this way:

• Dr. Jack Hayford's presentation is first, providing a full picture of the purpose and message of each book.

• Dr. Scott Bauer's lesson is second, affording a grasp of the relevancy of each book and revealing the Spirit's power as it unveils Jesus Himself.

- Dr. Jack Hamilton's lesson is third in each volume, presenting the practical lessons of each book.

By means of these three lessons, a comprehensive overview of a book (or books) of the Bible is presented in each study, so it can be truly gained, grasped, and applied.

TRIPLE TOOLS—SUPPORT RESOURCES

1. Each Bible book, and the studies as originally presented, will be available on audio cassettes. Because Pastor Hayford has been asked by a national distributor of audio Bibles to record the whole of the Scriptures in the New King James Version, the text being studied is on tape. These audio Bibles are being produced now, and each correlated reading will be released in conjunction with the "Bible Book-A-Month" program (Fall 1996 through Spring 1998).
2. Audio cassettes of the three lessons are also available with each study guide. So, the entire set of books (like this one in your hand), the full Bible on audio cassettes (NKJV), and the complete teachings by Drs. Hayford, Bauer, and Hamilton will become available as they are produced from month to month.
3. The above two join with each book (like this one) to complete the support resources for the "Bible Book-A-Month" studies. Additional resources, noted in each volume, may also be ordered by calling Living Way Ministries at 800-776-8180.

GENESIS:
THE KEY WORD IS "BEGINNINGS"

All kinds of beginnings are related in Genesis: the beginning of the universe, life, humanity, the sabbath, sin, redemption, sacrifice, marriage, family, death, cities, art, language, and literature.

KEY VERSES

"And I will put enmity between you and the woman, and between your seed and her Seed; He shall bruise your head, and you shall bruise His heel."
Genesis 3:15

"I will bless those who bless you, and I will curse him who curses you; and in you all the families of the earth shall be blessed." Genesis 12:3

KEY CHAPTER: GENESIS 15

The Abrahamic covenant, first mentioned in Genesis 12:1-3 and made official in Chapter 15:1-21, is central to all Scripture. Three promises are given to Israel:

- The promise of a great land—"from the river of Egypt to the great river, the River Euphrates" (15:8)
- The promise of a great nation—"and I will make your descendants as the dust of the earth" (13:16)
- The promise of a great blessing—"I will bless you and make your name great; and you shall be a blessing" (12:2).

INTRODUCING THE BIBLE BOOK OF
GENESIS

Author:	Traditionally Moses
Date:	About 1440 B.C.
Theme:	Beginnings
Key Words:	Create, Covenant, Genealogy

AUTHOR

Jewish tradition lists Moses as the author of Genesis and of the next four books. Together these books are called the Pentateuch. Jesus said, *"If you believed Moses, you would believe Me; for he wrote about Me"* (John 5:46). The Pentateuch itself depicts Moses as the writer. (See Exodus 17:14; 24:4; and Deuteronomy 31:24.)

DATE

The traditional date of the Exodus from Egypt is the mid-fifteenth century B.C. First Kings 6:1 states that Solomon began building the temple "in the four hundred and eightieth year after the children of Israel had come out of the land of Egypt." Solomon is thought to have begun construction about 960 B.C., dating the Exodus about 1440 B.C. So Moses wrote Genesis after 1440 B.C., during the forty years in the wilderness.

Travels of the
PATRIARCHS

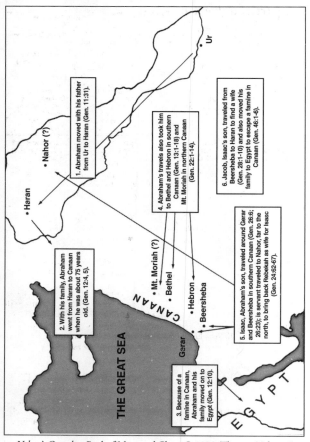

• Ur

1. Abraham moved with his father from Ur to Haran (Gen. 11:31).

• Nahor (?)

• Haran

4. Abraham's travels also took him to Bethel and Hebron in southern Canaan (Gen. 13:1-18) and Mt. Moriah in northern Canaan (Gen. 22:1-14).

6. Jacob, Isaac's son, traveled from Beersheba to Haran to find a wife (Gen. 28:1-10) and also moved his family to Egypt to escape a famine in Canaan (Gen. 46:1-6).

2. With his family, Abraham went from Haran to Canaan when he was about 75 years old. (Gen. 12:4, 5).

5. Isaac, Abraham's son, traveled around Gerar and Beersheba in southern Canaan (Gen. 26:6; 26:23); his servant traveled to Nahor, far to the north, to bring back Rebekah as wife for Isaac (Gen. 24:62-67).

• Mt. Moriah (?)
• Bethel
• Hebron
• Beersheba

Gerar

CANAAN

THE GREAT SEA

3. Because of a famine in Canaan, Abraham and his family moved on to Egypt (Gen. 12:10).

EGYPT

Nelson's Complete Book of Maps and Charts © 1993, Thomas Nelson, Inc.

PART 1

THE PILLAR PRINCIPLES OF GENESIS

JACK HAYFORD

GENESIS 10, 11
DESCENDANTS OF ADAM

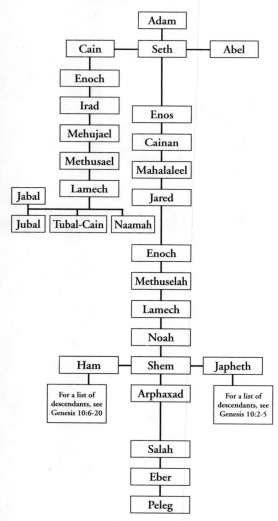

Adam

Cain — Seth — Abel

Enoch

Irad

Mehujael

Methusael

Lamech

Jabal

Jubal | Tubal-Cain | Naamah

Enos

Cainan

Mahalaleel

Jared

Enoch

Methuselah

Lamech

Noah

Ham — Shem — Japheth

For a list of descendants, see Genesis 10:6-20

Arphaxad

For a list of descendants, see Genesis 10:2-5

Salah

Eber

Peleg

The Pillar Principles of
GENESIS

"How It All Began" is how we have titled our three-part overview of the opening book of the Bible. There are more than simply obvious reasons for this designation. The first four words of the Book of Genesis are anything but a trite opening; they constitute an essential foundation point for wisdom.

"In the beginning, GOD…" is more than an introduction to His Word or His works of creation. Those words present *HIM—before all else, before the cosmos, before our galaxy, solar system or planet, before humanity.* The Bible introduces us to God as the One who IS—the I AM, the ever-present, before-and-beside-all-things, almighty, all-knowing One.

It is only in beginning with God, and with a clear identification of His person and nature that things in our world make sense and that purpose for our lives can be understood.

- It is not an accident that so much of mankind, blinded by sin, so diligently seeks to define creation without God as its source, because to do so is to be faced with the obvious need to acknowledge Him as *man's* fundamental point of dependence.

- It is not merely misfortune that, even with man's

best resources and efforts brought to bear, our world tumbles forward in confusion and teeters on destruction; but it's the inevitable by-product of rejecting the wisdom of acknowledging our world's Founder.

To study Genesis, and thereby gain an understanding of what the Bible is all about, is to lay the foundations for wisdom in our soul. It is in truly coming to understand "how it all began" that each of us may discover the reason for our own personal existence. To see God's person and nature, revealed in His words and actions at the beginning of our world, can open our vision to see how ready He is today to work in our personal lives.

So open this first book of the Bible: read it… listen to it read…immerse yourself in it. Capture the wisdom available in knowing "How It All Began…"

- How the world and the heavens began…
- How all plants, trees, creatures and mankind began…
- How beauty, blessing and God's benediction began…
- How sin and evil, pain and death first entered the race…
- How redemptive, restorative promise was first given…
- How a plan and purpose began to unfold, not only *to* mankind, but *through* us.

In beginning with the Book of Beginnings, anticipate the beginning of yet another reality in your own heart: *the gaining of wisdom born of heav-*

en-given knowledge through God's Word. For, "The fear of the Lord" (a reverence based in knowing who He is and how He works) is the *beginning* of knowledge (Prov. 1:7a). He will deepen and increase our capacity for steadfastness as well as growth in all of life. While the foolishness of unbelief despises the foundations which Genesis reveals, as we with living faith open to them, God Himself will respond in the very way He has promised in His Word:

> *"Surely I will pour out My spirit on you;*
> *I will make My words known to you."*
> Proverbs 1:23

GENESIS'
CENTRAL PERSONALITIES

There are three central personalities in the Book of Genesis. Each is introduced at a point of beginning, and the rest of the Bible unfolds on the basis of what *begins* with and is fathered by each of these.

GOD
- The *Beginner* of all things (1:1).
- The *Father* of creation, life, and promise (1:2-31; 3:15; 12:1-3).

ADAM
- The *beginning* of all mankind (2:7-25).
- The *father* of the human race (5:1-32),

sin (3:6, 7) and death (3:17-19—see also Romans 5:12-21).

ABRAHAM

- The *beginning* of God's covenant of promise (12:1-3; 17:4-8; 22:16-18).
- The *father* of the Jews (28:13, 14) and of God's way of faith (15:4-6—see also Romans 4:1-25).

Of course, many other key personalities are present in Genesis:

- Eve, the first woman and founding mother of humanity (1:26-28; 2:18-25; 3:20).
- Satan, first manifest in the serpent (3:1-5; see Revelation 12:9).
- The earliest patriarchs, including Enoch and Methuselah (5:1-32).
- Noah, an instrument of preserving the race (Ch. 6-10).
- Isaac and Rebecca, Jacob and his sons (Ch. 21-35).
- Ishmael and (through Isaac) Esau, Abraham's other key offspring (16:1-16; 21:1-21; 27:30-46; 28:6-9; 36:1-43).
- Joseph, a picture of redemptive instrumentality (Ch. 37-50).

However, as fine as the weave of Genesis' tapestry depicting the beginning of all things, including redemption's plans, the foundational revelation of God's purpose and plan for mankind is unfolded in the three—God, Adam, and Abraham. Our goal in this overview is to capture the great themes—the *pillar principles* and *towering truths* that are found in

Genesis—which reveal three things:

- God's person—noting His power and purpose in Creation;
- Man's design—noting his disobedience and sin's destructiveness.
- Abraham's call unto God's plan, promise, and purposed role.

To understand these three concepts is to avoid the majority of detours that lead to human intellectual and spiritual confusion. Most error begins with wrong thinking about God, man, and redemption. A straight-view of Genesis lays the foundation for a clear-view of life.

I. GENESIS REVEALS GOD'S PERSON.

There are four primary facts or traits about God that are clearly set forth in Genesis: God as Creator, as Lover, as Judge, as Redeemer.

A. God as Creator.

From this we derive insight into God's nature as (a) Pre-existent (being *before* all things), (b) Immanent (omni-present), (c) Almighty (omnipotent), (d) All-knowing (omniscient), (e) Transcendent (*beyond* His creation)—in contrast to pantheism's "God *is* or *is within* nature." All these things are seen in Creation (Psalm 19:1-6) and man is accountable to this natural revelation (Romans 1:18-31).

1. Genesis 1 reveals God as the Founder of all Creation. What are the significant implications in this?

      a.   Spiritually, that we worship, honor, and obey Him.

      b.   Intellectually, that we accept by faith His purpose and power, though others by faith believe in purposeless force.

2.   In creation, we see God's methods of "bringing into being." He is never obstructed by the difficulties or dynamics of evil or of confusion.

      a.   He moves by His Spirit.

      b.   He speaks His Word.

His creativity has order and design. There is a natural progress of unfolding beauty. There is consistent "dividing" that serves the wholeness of the whole. There is always a breath of life in His work. If His style and spirit as Creator is a worthy model for us in our creativity, what could this imply?

B. God as Love.

"Love" is the one attribute of God that is said to define Him (1 John 4:16), whereas all other attributes are spoken *of* Him or noted *about* Him. There is much evidence of His nature as "Love" in Genesis.

1.   Love is revealed in the desire of the Godhead to create a being "in our image and likeness" (1:26-28). The obvious objective is to share in a partnership of mutual care and trust. Divine love is overwhelmingly unselfish and desires to extend and expand its every resource to others.

2.   Love is revealed in the creative fashioning

of a "helper comparable to him" (Adam—2:18-25). The method and manner in which this action is taken reveals a tender sensitivity directed at revealing itself to both the man and the woman in this act.

3. Love is revealed in the instant motivation to answer self-inflicted punishment (on mankind's part) with an immediate provision to cover the shame of sin's intrusion (3:21), and with a long-range promise to break sin's penalty (3:15).

God's love is a *supernatural revelation* and out-pouring of Himself (Romans 5:5), not a "natural resource" available on demand by humankind. Popular theology fails to link love to God's Word, where it is shown (as above) rooted in (1) His purpose for humans, (2) His call to the sanctity of marriage vows, and (3) His terms and provision for redemption.

In contrast, human philosophies of "God's love" define (a) human purpose on the basis of human whim, (b) marriage commitment on the basis of emotional transiency, and (c) redemption from sin on the basis of arbitrary religious opinion.

C. God as Judge.

Abraham defines God's righteousness as just, saying, "Shall not the Judge of all the earth do right?" His rhetorical question presumes the answer, "Absolutely YES—Of course!" To live in any generation is to hear God's goodness impugned constantly, as though He is to blame for life's injustices. But *earth's human failures* are no argument against God's justice or kindness. Genesis reveals God's ways as Judge of all morally responsible beings He has created.

1. See His merciful judgment, even in the wake of human rebellion and sin (3:1-24).

2. See His warning away from judgment, even though Cain refuses the warning (4:7). See His insistence upon remembering the cost of sin, and refusing to allow a man to write his own "rules." As Judge, He exacts the payment justice requires, not impulsively, but consistent with the cosmic order (4:3, 4). Even then, mercy accompanies Cain's self-induced judgment (4:13-15).

3. See His provision to escape from judgment. Even though justice requires the inevitability of the judgment, He seeks to make a way for those accepting His grace (Mark—6:1-22).

4. See His motivation in judgment, in "cleansing from evil" in order that a new era might be born (The Flood—6:1-13; Sodom and Gomorrah—18:16-19:29; the Amorites—15:16).

God reveals immediate and direct action in judgment. He never compromises the righteousness of His rule, yet He never surrenders the mercy with which He exercises His judgment. (Make your own list of Genesis' events where God exercises quick justice, but with mercy.)

D. God as Redeemer.

The foremost trait of God's self-revelation in

the Bible, and the central message of His Word, is His desire to redeem—to bring back what is lost, to restore, to recover, to reconcile.

1. Rather than leave mankind in his dilemma of death, He announces a program of redemption (3:15).

2. Rather than display His power to penalize, He relentlessly chooses a pathway of provision and mercy (6:3).

3. Rather than sustain the original curse on the ground (3:17), God demonstrates His recovering, reconciling ways by removing that curse following the Flood (8:21,22).

4. He shows His desire to heal and recover from even those results of judgment due to violation of His ways (20:1-18).

5. He gives a master-type lesson in His intent to ultimately provide a redeemer, in His call to Abraham (Chap. 22). (Do your own comparative study: in how may ways can you see the way God gave His only Son forecast when He called Abraham to present Isaac in sacrifice?)

With a biblical foundation of sound *theology* (the study of God), all that ensues in life not only stands on good footings, but can be built upon. In the light of God's Person, let us look at "man."

II. GENESIS REVEALS MAN'S PURPOSE AND CONDITION.

Anthropology is the study of man (Gk. *anthropos*),

and in the book of Genesis there are four primary facts that are revealed. To miss understanding them is to become vulnerable to philosophical notions which are born of human pride and presumption. To understand them is to find the liberating truth that sets free the possibility that each person can realize the highest possibilities of their humanness and personhood.

A. Though a created being, and thereby subject to His rule, man has been created with a double dignity:

1. The nobility of being made in God's image and likeness, with an endless capacity for being, an expansive capacity for creativity, and an enviable capacity for procreation (1:26).

2. The regal possibilities of humankind are intended as promised "dominion" (1:28) and realized through obedient submission (2:15-17). As a moral being, the glorious essence of humankind's possibilities is dependent upon our abiding within the decrees (framework) of our intended being.

B. Man was created for and intended to know an incredibly granted partnership with the Creator in overseeing the affairs of earth (Psalm 8). Therefore man is of inestimable worth in the mind and heart of God (Hebrews 2:1-18).

1. This explains the pre-creation, pre-incarnation agreement within the Godhead (Psalm 40:7; Hebrews 10:5-7; Matthew 25:34;

Ephesians 1:4; 1 Peter 1:18-21;
Revelation 13:8).

2. This "partnership," which through sin has violated trust in the only One capable of making it successful, explains the condition of the broken affairs of earth and mankind (Psalm 115:16).

C. Man has broken the "natural law," having become a violator of God's trust, put himself in conflict with God's decrees, and been disobedient to the terms of his place in the created order.

1. We are without defense for any part we play in human patterns of sinning (Romans1:18-32), irrespective of how inconsequential we may judge our violative behavior to be.

2. Examine the list of human habits and failures in the Romans passage mentioned in #1, and let the severity of this issue settle in your heart and mind.

D. Man's only hope is in the manifest nature of God to love, to redeem at His expense, to reconcile us to fellowship with Him, and to restore His intended dominion in our lives.

1. Review the issues of God as Redeemer, above. Rejoice in and receive His grace and forgiveness in Christ (John 3:16, Ephesians 1:3-7; 2:1-10; 1 John 1:1-10).

2. What are areas of "lost dominion" in your life, which you would like to invite God's grace to restore?

III. GENESIS INTRODUCES THE LIFE OF FAITH.

With the magnificence of God's love and redemptive ways introduced, the book of Genesis shows the first steps in His plan to reach the world. He selects a man, calls him to His purpose as He issues great promises He will fulfill if the man will respond in faith. Abram (later called Abraham) is that man, and with him, God introduces two things:

- The pathway by which faith is begun, learned and grown in; and
- The person who becomes the human fountainhead through which a "people" of redemptive purpose are begotten.

A. Abraham is presented in both the Old and New Testaments as the father of a "natural seed" and a "spiritual seed."

1. The natural seed will become *physical/political* Israel, with promise of a geographic "land" (13:14-18). This is the Jewish people, who fulfill a highly significant redemptive purpose as Abraham's natural seed (Romans 9:3-5).

2. The spiritual seed will become a people through whom all mankind shall be blessed. This is a mix of *both* Jews and Gentiles (Gen. 12:1-3; Gal. 3:6-9). The spiritual seed are the inheritors of "the promise"—the life revealing God's recovered, intended purpose for His redeemed

among mankind—reborn, renewed, filled with His Spirit, and living in His Kingdom possibilities (Galatians 3:13-18, 29; Romans 4, 5).

B. Abraham is the pioneer of a walk in worship and faith that moves beyond the failures and foibles of the flesh and, however imperfect the human vessel or human understanding is at times, God's promised purposes are still realized.

1. Abraham's life covers fourteen chapters in the book of Genesis—chapters 11:27-25:11. Make your own outline of his chief moments of obedience, his notable instances of failure. What was God's response to each? How do these lessons apply to you?

2. Abraham's life is a succession of "altar experiences." Some include direct mention of an altar (e.g. 12:7; 12:8; 13:4; 13:18; 22:1-19), while others do not, even though they are distinct worship or prayer experiences (e.g. 15:1-18; 18:16-33). Trace these and determine what this "pathway of prayer and worship" may hold for you, in its lesson symbolized in Abraham's experience.

THE LIFE OF
JACOB

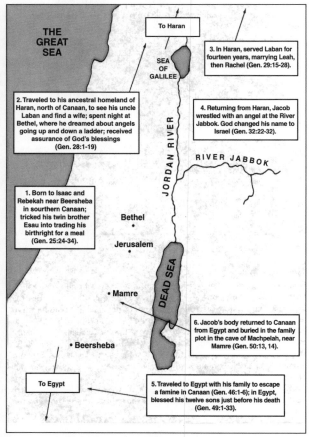

THE GREAT SEA

To Haran

SEA OF GALILEE

3. In Haran, served Laban for fourteen years, marrying Leah, then Rachel (Gen. 29:15-28).

2. Traveled to his ancestral homeland of Haran, north of Canaan, to see his uncle Laban and find a wife; spent night at Bethel, where he dreamed about angels going up and down a ladder; received assurance of God's blessings (Gen. 28:1-19)

4. Returning from Haran, Jacob wrestled with an angel at the River Jabbok. God changed his name to Israel (Gen. 32:22-32).

JORDAN RIVER

RIVER JABBOK

1. Born to Isaac and Rebekah near Beersheba in southern Canaan; tricked his twin brother Esau into trading his birthright for a meal (Gen. 25:24-34).

Bethel

Jerusalem

DEAD SEA

• Mamre

6. Jacob's body returned to Canaan from Egypt and buried in the family plot in the cave of Machpelah, near Mamre (Gen. 50:13, 14).

• Beersheba

To Egypt

5. Traveled to Egypt with his family to escape a famine in Canaan (Gen. 46:1-6); in Egypt, blessed his twelve sons just before his death (Gen. 49:1-33).

Nelson's Complete Book of Maps and Charts © 1993, Thomas Nelson, Inc.

PART 2

THE RELEVANT ANSWERS IN GENESIS

SCOTT BAUER

THE TABLE OF NATIONS

Shem, Ham and Japheth became the fathers
of the nations. (Genesis 10:1-32)

Shem: The Semitic peoples —
Jews, Arabs, Babylonians, Assyrians, Arameans,
Phoenicians.

Ham: The Hamitic peoples —
Ethiopians, Egyptians, Canaanites, Philistines,
possibly the African and Oriental peoples, though many
scholars view the Orientals as Japhetic.

Japheth: The Japhetic peoples —
the Medes, Greeks, Cypriots, etc. Probably the Caucasian
people of Europe and of northern Asia. Many scholars
would also include the Orientals here.

THE SONS OF JACOB

The sons born to Leah:
Reuben—*(see, a son)* (29:32)
Simeon—*(hearing)* (29:33)
Levi—*(joined)* (29:34)
Judah—*(praise)* (29:35)
Issachar—*(hire)* (30:18)
Zebulun—*(dwelling)* (30:20)

The sons born to Bilhah, the handmaid of Rachel:
Dan—*(judge)* (30:6)
Naphtali—*(wrestling)* (30:8)

The sons born to Zilpah, handmaid of Leah:
Gad—*(a troop or good fortune)* (30:11)
Asher—*(happy)* (30:13)

The sons born to Rachel:
Joseph—*(adding)* (30:24)
Benjamin—*(son of the right hand)* (35:18)

ANSWERING QUESTIONS AND
SOLVING PROBLEMS

How did the world come into being? Science has theories. The Bible has answers. However, the controversy has swirled around this question of our ultimate beginnings. Searching the edge of the universe, scientists attempt to peer into the past and secure some rational explanation for all that is around us. The Bible simply reports the facts of God's personal creative action: "In the beginning God created the heavens and the earth" (Genesis 1:1).

The scientific community is often found arguing against the existence of God, and yet it finds no contradiction in proposing that the whole of the universe was once a single mass of matter detonated in the "big bang." They theorize that the entire universe came from this single mass as acted upon by the laws of physics. They make no reasonable explanation for the source of such a mass, nor do they answer the question of the source of these laws of physics. These scholars make a purely theological assertion that matter is pre-existent (always having been, and not created) and that there is no architect of the physical laws which govern our world. Psalm 14:1 answers the scoffer who rejects the notion that there is no God.

However, reasonable people who do believe in a loving, all-powerful God as the source of creation often have substantial questions about how the universe began. Genesis 1 informs us of what happened at creation in rather vague generalities. One of the uses of the Hebrew word *bara*—"created" in Genesis 1:1—is for a unique kind of creation. It can be used for creation "ex nihilo"—from nothing. Genesis 1:1 also offers an explanation of the eternal God Himself beginning the work of creation. In verse two, the Holy Spirit is at work "hovering over the face of the deep." And in the remainder of the chapter, God "speaks" and creative things happen. Apart from these broad descriptions, the details of this process of creation are uncertain.

There are a number of very significant questions which deserve thoughtful and reasonable answers about creation. What does the Bible say about the age of the earth? What does the Bible say about the theory of Darwinian evolution to explain the differentiation of the species? Does the Bible teach that the earth was created in seven 24-hour days?

HOW DID CREATION HAPPEN?

For those who desire to be honest with the biblical account of creation, there are certain conditions which must be met in evaluating the possible theories of creation. First, according to Genesis 1, it must be plausible. Second, it must be consistent with what other portions of the Bible observe to be true concerning creation. Third, it must be consistent with our knowledge of God and His ways. For many, a theory of creation must be intellectually feasible in light of the scientific data we possess concerning the history of the earth. There are three general scenarios for creation that fit the Bible text of Genesis 1, and two of these fit the accepted scientific geological evidence of the earth.

THE "LITERAL" SEVEN-DAY THEORY

This theory demands a literal interpretation of the seven-day creation theory. God created the universe and all in it in seven 24-hour days. The same people who believe this theory often attempt to calculate the date of creation by this same literal approach. By adding the total number of generations, as provided by the genealogies in Scripture, and linking them to historically certain biblical dates, they arrive at the year of Adam's creation. Generally, the date 4004 B.C. has been calculated by this method.

There are obvious challenges to this theory. The use of the word "day" throughout Scripture does not always refer to a 24-hour period of time. Second Peter 3:8 declares, "A day is as a thousand years, and a thousand years as a day." The use of the phrase "day of the Lord" in Scripture does not require its being a single day. So, the literal interpretation of a 24-hour period for a day is imposed on the text by this theory.

If the earth began in 4004 B.C. there are a number of difficult scientific questions which beg to be answered. How do we explain the observed geological ages in the earth? What about dinosaurs and the ice ages in continents? Since we understand the process at work in places like the Grand Canyon, how could all that have been done in only 6000 years? The inability of the literal theory to deal effectively with these questions severely limits its believability.

DAY/AGE THEORY

This theory suggests that the "days" of Genesis 1 are really geologic periods. This would explain the scientific observation of an earth that is billions of years old. Without the limits of a very young earth, as proposed above, there is no need to sacrifice the scientific opinions about how the processes which have shaped the earth could have happened.

This theory also allows for another theory concerning Genesis 1. Evolution has been proposed by many scientists as the answer for the differentiation of species. By proposing a single common ancestor which resulted from a bio-chemical reaction in the primordial oceans of the earth, scientists have sought to explain creation without God. Though this does not answer the theological question of the causation of the universe, it is an attempt to answer the biological questions of beginnings. Many believers have embraced the theory of evolution. Though there is no fossil record of the transmutation of species, evolutionists contend that eventually such fossil records will be found.

A particular form of this theory has been dubbed "Theistic Evolution." This theory proposes that evolution was a God-ordained miracle in the creation story. The "miracle" of evolution, according to this theory, is that God personally supervised the process of evolution. Though we cannot observe a "transmutation" of species in our world today, nor in the fossil record of history, nonetheless, God used evolution in Genesis 1 to bring about creation.

This theory certainly argues against the very character and nature of God as a personal creator. And the witness of Genesis 2 in the creation of Adam must then be "mythologized" in order to be accepted. The Day/Age Theory is often cited by believers to explain creation. However, it is not universally believed.

THE GAP THEORY

In an attempt to synthesize the Bible record of Genesis 1 & 2 with the scientific observations of the age of the earth, the Gap theory has been proposed. According to this theory, Genesis 1:1 and 1:2 are different accounts of creation. There is a "gap" of time between them. The construction of the Hebrew in these passages is quite different.

As observed already, *bara* is the Hebrew word for "create" in Genesis 1:1. This word incorporates the concept of creation from nothing. However, in Genesis 1:2 the Holy Spirit was "hovering" over the creation that was void. Some scholars believe the Hebrew grammar allows the interpretation of "void" to be rendered "was made void." The Hebrew word translated "without form" can also be translated "confusion." According to the Gap theory, the earth was in a state of chaotic darkness and was rendered void as a result. Here the darkness is not merely the absence of physical light, but also the presence of spiritual darkness.

This theory seeks to explain the scriptures which refer to the earth's "pre-history." Jesus saw Satan "fall like lightning from heaven" (Luke 10:18). Isaiah 14 and Ezekiel 28 are believed by many scholars to offer a picture of the satanic fall from heaven in a rebellion against God. Revelation 12:7 describes a heavenly war between the rebellious angels that followed Satan and the hosts of heaven who remained faithful to God. The devil "was cast to the earth, and his angels were cast out with him" (Revelation 12:9). This action pre-dates Genesis 1:2 according to the Gap theory. Due to the cataclysmic fallout from the heavenly rebellion, the earth was "rendered void" (Genesis 1:2).

According to the theory, innumerable years passed between Genesis 1:1 and 1:2. The trauma of this spiritual invasion of darkness would have required God's action to restore the earth in Genesis1:2. This theory provides for the geological ages which scientists observe, and coordinate with evidence of a cataclysmic change in the earth and its environment.

All three theories—the Seven Day Literal, Day/Age, and Gap are embraced by sincere believers. One thing is certain—God did the creating, supernaturally. And, when He was done it was "very good" (Genesis 1:31).

ARE THERE TWO STORIES OF CREATION IN GENESIS 1 AND 2?

This question observes the significant differences in the style, content, and even the names of

God between Genesis 1:1-2:3 and Genesis 2:4-25. In the first chapter, God's name is the Hebrew word *Elohim*—the great, almighty God. This is the all-powerful God of creation whose name is used in a loftier poetic style. This is the God to be feared. His name is plural, in an intensive sense, and it is the story of this Creator God that Moses tells in Genesis 1.

In Exodus 3:14, Moses (the author of Genesis—Joshua 8:31-32) changes the name of God to the Hebrew word *Yahweh*. This is the intimate, personal name of "I AM." He is the God who is present in the lives of His people. He is the God of salvation and redemption who loves His people and interacts with them. This is the covenant-making God who will ultimately reveal Himself to Abram to begin the process of reaching to humanity (Genesis 12:3). He is also the God who will meet Moses on the mountain with the Law, and, finally, He is our Savior, sparing no expense to rescue humanity from sin and destruction.

In Genesis 2:4-25, the creation event is told through an understanding of this God Moses has come to know intimately (Ex. 33:11). Some have suggested that these two chapters of Genesis were proof of two different documents written by some-one other than Moses. However, these misunder-stand the nature of a relationship with the Lord which acknowledges His splendor, majesty, and awesome power, and at the same time experiences His personal, loving attention to all the details of our lives. Moses knows this God who is <u>both</u> *Elohim* and *Yahweh*. And he wants all who read this book to know the one and true God as well.

Jesus Revealed in
GENESIS

The book of Genesis has occurrences of the Lord Jesus in it. Obviously, the name "Jesus" is not used. But, clearly the Lord is found in text as the God who comes to earth and interacts with His people. Jesus appears in Genesis during the creation event as second member of the God-head. Though He is not directly referred to in this manner, His presence is obvious and corroborated by other texts of Scripture. There are also at least three distinct accounts of theophanies (where God appears) in Genesis at critical moments in the lives of the Patriarchs. Many scholars believe these to be pre-incarnate appearances of Christ.

CHRIST
AT CREATION

The name of God is plural in Genesis 1— *Elohim*. This is a plural which intensifies our understanding of God, adding to the majesty of His Person. However, that is not all it is in this chapter. In verse 26, God is quoted as talking to Himself, "Let Us make man in Our image, according to Our likeness." This text makes perfect sense as we understand God interacting as Father, Son, and Holy Spirit (Matthew 28:19). In the act of creation, the triune Godhead insists on making man in a fashion which allows for relationship, interaction, and the spiritual capacity for fellowship with the Creator.

Jesus was present and active in the creation of

man (John 1:3), knowing full well our human potential for eternal relationship with Him and the fact of sin that would break that fellowship. Scripture teaches us that the Lord knew not only the facts of the human failure at Creation—but also our own personal failure as individuals. The decision about Calvary and Jesus' death on the Cross occurred before the Creation event, not after (Revelation 13:8). And, Jesus' knowledge of us personally and the provision for our salvation pre-dates Genesis 1 and the Creation event (Ephesians 1:4-7).

The enormous love of God that calculated and paid for the cost of relationship with humanity, even before Creation, reveals to us the heart of God. From the opening scene of Scripture, God's purpose toward us is clear. He wants relationship with His creation and with each of us personally—and He has spared no expense to make it possible.

CHRIST AT THE SACRIFICE
Genesis 15:17

God is making covenant with Abram, assuring him of promise of an inheritance. In this passage, Abram has prepared a sacrifice for the Lord. After the sacrifice is placed on the altar, something highly unusual takes place. Abram waits for an extended time without anything happening at the altar. Finally, after sundown, a "smoking oven" (the Lord Himself) is seen passing between the pieces of the sacrifice on the altar. God is committing Himself to covenant with this man, and it pre-figures the sacrifice Jesus will make "once for all" (Hebrews 10:10).

CHRIST REAFFIRMS
THE PROMISE
Genesis 18:14

Three men come to visit Abraham and Sarah
verse 2. Two of them are angels (Genesis 19:1) and,
according to 18:14, the other is the Lord Himself.
Despite the circumstance of Abraham and Sarah's
advancing age and the human impossibility of bear-
ing a child, the Lord reaffirms His promise to bless
them. It is another occasion of the physical revealing
of the Lord before the incarnation.

Yahweh, the Lord God, restates His promise.
He is about to bless Abraham and Sarah, though
they are stretched beyond their own ability to have
faith for a child. In Genesis 17:17, Abraham laughs
at the notion that a child will come to a 100-year-
old man and his 90-year-old wife. Sarah "laughed
within her" in 18:12. The nagging doubts about our
own ability to produce anything in our own strength
do not limit the God who has promised to work in us.

CHRIST
ENCOUNTERS JACOB
Genesis 32:24-31

Jacob's wrestling match is with "a Man" verse 24.
In Hosea 12:4, we are told it was "the Angel" of the
Lord who struggled with Jacob. It is in this contest
of wills that three things take place.

First, Jacob struggles with God at a crossroad
moment in his life. He fears meeting his estranged
twin brother who has promised to kill him for steal-
ing the blessing of their father (Genesis 27:41). He
is unable to escape this encounter with Esau, and

has no hope of resisting the power of his brother and the four hundred men who accompany him (Genesis 33:1).

Second, following the struggle, the Lord changes Jacob's name to Israel. "Prince with God" is the meaning of this new name. This is a radical departure from the meaning of Jacob—"deceiver." Having struggled with God, Jacob has experienced a transformation that is so fundamental to his life that only a new name will suffice to describe it. In fact, every believer in Jesus Christ is promised a new name (Rev. 2:17). No longer will we be referred to by anything that reminds us of the old nature and character. We are new creatures in Christ with a new name to go with our transformed nature and character.

Third, following the wrestling match, the Lord touched Israel's hip, dislocating it so that he walked with a limp the rest of his life. The obvious lesson is that once we have wrestled with God in our own lives, we will never walk the same again. Not only will our gait be changed, but it will be apparent to others as well.

The presence of Jesus in Genesis illustrates a truth that is found consistently throughout the Bible. God is interested in people. From the very beginning of Creation the Lord has desired a relationship with humanity. "Let Us make man in Our Image" (1:26) is a profound statement confirming the value God places on us. And, in the subsequent occasions of discovering Christ in this first book of the Bible, there is a thoroughgoing concern for the details of our relationship with Him. The Lord has gone beyond the boundaries of heaven to seek out His creation. Our response to Him in faith is all that is necessary to fulfill the relationship God desires to have with us.

THE HOLY SPIRIT
AT WORK IN POWER

Specific reference occurs to the Holy Spirit in Genesis only three times: at Creation in 1:2, in witness to man's wickedness in 6:3, and by a pagan king observing God at work in Joseph's life in 41:38. This is by no means the limit to the Holy Spirit's activities in the book.

Many of the phrases referring to the Lord "speaking" are not necessarily to be understood that people heard God's voice as an incarnate representation of God the Father or God the Son. God the Holy Spirit speaks to people as well and throughout Genesis we discover the development of a very personal relationship of God with His people. This intimacy is sustained by a sense of God's directing presence at crucial moments in the lives of the Patriarchs who are referred to in the book.

It, once again, establishes a pattern found in Genesis that will be found in the rest of the Bible: God reveals Himself to His people. God's supernatural intervention takes place in the lives of real people throughout the book—and it is still happening the same way today.

THE HOLY SPIRIT
IN CREATION

Genesis begins with a profound work of the Holy Spirit. Clearly, the God-head is at work in Creation. "In the beginning God created the heavens and the earth" (Gen. 1:1). We realize in John 1:2, that Jesus was present at Creation as the *Logos*, "Word" of God. And, "all things were made through Him" (John 1:3). However, as we review the Creation event in Gen. 1:3, the role of the Holy Spirit in bringing into being the will of God is absolutely essential.

The world was a roaring, churning mass of waters according to verse 2; it was over these waters that the Holy Spirit "was hovering." Quite to the contrary of the formless chaos, God the Holy Spirit began to fashion a world that was spoken into existence by God Himself. We do not understand completely the process by which the Father, Son, and Holy Spirit conjoined to create the world. The Holy Spirit's work of transformation from empty confusion to a magnificently ordered universe and planet is obvious even today, in a world that has been damaged by sin and humankind's failure to steward his responsibilities over the earth.

God spoke and the world came into being. The energy of God's Word under the "hovering" influence of the Holy Spirit is the ultimate power in creation. The Lord did not use pre-existent matter to build a world. The world was built on God's Word alone.

This opens the door to a vitally significant point which is present throughout God's history in dealing with humankind. Whenever God's people obey God's Word and submit to the work of the Holy Spirit, there is unbounded blessing and creativity. Under such circumstances not only is God able to do a creative new work in the lives of people, He is also free to work redemptively in areas of life which have been damaged by disobedience and sin. The spiritual principle outlined in Genesis 1 cannot be escaped: obey God's Word and surrender to the work of the Holy Spirit, and experience the miracle touch of God in your life (1 John 3:24).

This point is further elaborated in Genesis 1:7-8. The interesting use of the word "firmament" describes heaven in verse 7. The dry land is called "earth" in verse 8. The concept of firmament is more clearly understood as it is used in Psalm 150:1. "Firmament" is one of the places in which God is to be praised. The New English Bible renders this phrase in a unique and poetic way—but it offers a profound insight into the concept. "Praise Him in the vault of heaven, in the vault of His power." The firmament is the place wherein true power resides.

That is why Jesus is insistent in Matthew 6:10 that we pray, "Your kingdom come, Your will be done on earth as it is in heaven." The heavenly pattern is the form to which the things on earth are to conform. And, it takes people who bear the conviction that the spiritual realm is the final authority for earthly matters, and who take seriously their role in prayer. By partnering with the Holy Spirit as we pray, we invade the realm of the "dry land" with the resource found in the "firmament" of heaven.

The presence of the Holy Spirit in Creation

opens our understanding to the truly spiritual dimension of the world around us. This spiritual world is repeatedly witnessed in Genesis following creation. God breaks into the realm of ordinary people with supernatural power from above.

THE HOLY SPIRIT'S WORK IN PEOPLE

It is not practical to identify all of the places the Holy Spirit works with power in people's lives throughout Genesis. But highlighted are instances of ways the Spirit works with people.

Cain is confronted with sin—4:6-15. The Holy Spirit's warning in verse 7 is terrifyingly clear, "sin lies at the door. And its desire is for you, but you should rule over it." The Lord is not only identifying the potential for trouble but announcing its presence. First Corinthians 10:13 warns of temptation, but also promises a God-given way of escape. The Holy Spirit's warning to Cain was ignored at great loss.

Noah prepared for judgment—6:13-9:17. Noah was warned of impending disaster, and instructed on the manner by which his family would be saved. Its relevance to us today is obvious (1 Peter 3:20-21). However, the Lord did more than simply warn Noah. Noah was convinced of the reality of the coming judgment (John 16:8). Though the Bible records no rain falling previously, Noah is told to build an enormous boat on dry land. The operation of faith is more than merely a man's believing. It is God's assisting Noah grasp something beyond his comprehension (1 Corinthians 12:9). Specific directions for the ark were given.

Nelson's Complete Book of Maps and Charts © 1993, Thomas Nelson, Inc.

The 100 years that Noah was engaged in building were sustained by faith. The encouraging, directing work of the Spirit is obvious in this man's life.

Hagar spared from death—21:17-21. The cry of a thirsty boy and a desperate single mother are answered by the Lord, not according to their faith, but according to their need. With a miracle of divine provision, Hagar and Ishmael are saved, and the boy receives assurances of God's purpose for his life. The delivering grace that spared and encouraged them is a distinct work of the Holy Spirit. Though outside the line of spiritual succession, Ishmael is nonetheless blessed by the covenant-keeping God who promised to bless Abraham's offspring.

Abraham discovers a ram—22:12-13. At the point of absolute surrender to God, in faith the Lord provides a substitute for the sacrifice of Isaac. A miracle provision occurs through a divine revelation to Abraham of what he did not see before. This is a direct intervention of God assisting a man who was living in obedience to his own understanding of God's purpose. It is in this context that the Holy Spirit met and provided for him.

Isaac receives a bride—24:1-67. Rebekah is brought to Isaac as a bride through a remarkable set of prayers and circumstances which are by no means coincidental—but rather God-directed. Abraham's servant is directed by gifts of knowledge and wisdom in fulfilling the task to return with a wife for his master (1 Cor-inthians 12:8). This is reminiscent of specific and unusual directions given to Ananias as the Lord directed him to serve Saul in Acts 9:11-12.

Joseph interprets a dream—41:1-57. The Holy Spirit gives Joseph a supernatural knowledge and wisdom concerning both the content of Pharoah's dream and an appropriate course of action to take as a result. The obvious supernatural nature of the wisdom of God revealed is acknowledged by the pagan king—"Can we find such a one as this—a man in whom is the Spirit of God?"

Israel prophesies over his sons—49:1-28. As Israel speaks a prophecy over his sons, there is a direct correlation to the power of those prophecies that is measured four hundred years later as Moses and the nation of Israel have left Egypt, and the tribes are numbered (Numbers 1:19-49). The Lord confirms the prophetic declaration of Israel, and in accordance with it, the two largest tribes at the Exodus are: (1) Judah, and (2) Joseph (Ephraim and Manasseh combined). These two boys are given the highest commendation by their father Israel 400 years earlier. However, "Benajmin is a ravenous wolf; in the morning he shall devour the prey, and at night he shall divide the spoil"—this according to his father's prophecy in 49:27. This harsh prophetic word is confirmed as the tribe of Benjamin is by far the smallest of all the tribes at the Exodus. This incident illustrates the power of our words to bless and to curse as we partner with the Lord. The Holy Spirit performs the Lord's Word and confirms in the experience of His people.

The power of the Spirit to inform, bless, warn, comfort, and do the miraculous is revealed in Genesis, and is the way of God in all the Bible. God's power and person are available to His people who live by faith, and seek to walk sensitively to His leading. The personal attention God gives to His people is never more obvious than when the Holy Spirit pours out grace in the lives of individuals so that they are able to know God and respond to His goodness.

PART 3

PRACTICAL WISDOM FROM GENESIS

JACK HAMILTON

The Nations of
GENESIS

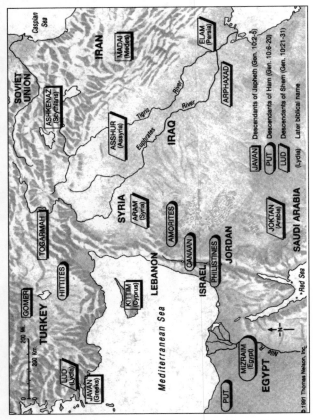

Nelson's Complete Book of Maps and Charts © 1993, Thomas Nelson, Inc.

RELATIONAL LIVING IN THE
COVENANTS

The Bible as a whole is God's self-disclosure. He is making Himself and His ways known to people. God doesn't *need* relationship with humans—He *wants* it. God's interaction with His creation is for the good of creation and not because He has a relational void. God is completely self-sustained and self-fulfilled. It is His love of people that motivates His desire to interact with them. And when people respond positively to the LORD'S overtures, they are blessed and stabilized.

Thus a secondary purpose for the Bible emerges. It is an accurate account of God's historic relationship with people. The Scriptures record how this interface of the Creator with the creature began, how it was rent, and how it was restored.

THE RELATIONAL MODEL

The model for relationship is found in the Godhead. The completeness of how this mystery works is amazing. The main reason, up to this point in time, that humans are befuddled by the Holy Trinity is there is nothing like it on earth. While God is a single unit, He is best understood by three co-existent manifestations.

Confusion arises as to how this is possible without having three identical persons or three gods instead of One. When it is understood that the Creator is not duplicated in creation, the immensity of this amazing relationship in the Godhead begins to unfold. God's essence is single, but the manifestation of His person and His interaction with creation is multiple.

An illustration might be helpful in beginning to appreciate the awesome nature of God. The chemical formula of water is two parts hydrogen and one part oxygen (H_2O). This element of nature maintains this design always; however, it may take different forms. If frozen, it becomes ice (a solid); if left alone between the temperatures of 32° and 212° Fahrenheit, it is liquid; but heat it beyond 212°, and it becomes steam (a gas). While the manifestation is different and has different functions, the essence— its chemical makeup—is not changed.

The external nature of the Godhead is a reflection of the internal dynamic. The function of personality exists in the manifestation of the Father, the Son, and the Holy Spirit. There is absolute truth in their relationship; therefore, there is absolute trust. There is absolute holiness in their relationship and, because of this, ultimate joy is known among them. Because love is fundamental in their being, the Godhead serves one another. Since there is no competition among them, there is absolute completion in all they do. The moral essence and life of God is what He shared with humans in creating them.

RELATIONSHIP AT THE CORE

On the sixth day, when man was created, God

made possible the relationship between Himself and Adam. There was stewardship responsibility assigned, authority invested, and accountability required. The relationship and its expressions were possible because in creating Adam the essence of his life was the spirit breathed by God into him. Since God is Spirit, the interaction between God and Adam would be executed spiritually. The relationship that Adam had with God formed the value of his being. It wasn't how well he performed his duty that satisfied his soul, but the encounters with God which deepened with intimacy on each occasion. They talked together and walked together. It was an echo of the relationship among the members of the Godhead.

The wisdom of God called for Adam to give names to all the creatures and beasts that had been created. This was not just some busy work given to Adam by God, but became the way that Adam understood his creation was incomplete. God declared, "It is not good that man should be alone; I will make a helper comparable to him" (2:18).

God causes Adam to sleep and removes from him the material from which woman is created. The significance of this method of creation is that it afforded the relationship of man and woman to be on equal footing. Adam seems to comprehend this reality when he exclaims, "This is now bone of my bone and flesh of my flesh; she shall be called Woman, because she was taken out of Man" (2:23). The Bible goes on to report that the relationship between the pair would be based on their unity, commitment to each other, and their acceptance of one another (2:24, 25). Their union was so complete that a single name sufficed for them—Adam (5:2).

This imagery of relationship mirrored that of the Godhead as much as possible in material form. There would not be another fully complete form of this kind of relationship until Jesus would declare, "I and My Father are One" (John 10:30).

THE DEATH BLOW
TO RELATIONSHIPS

The Bible account reports what was meant to last was torn and severed. Genesis, Chapter 3 describes how the relationship was broken. It is fair to say that the health of the relationship between the couple was based on the wholeness of their relationship with God. The seduction to disobey the commandment concerning eating the fruit of the Tree of the Knowledge of Good and Evil is the first strain on the relationship between God and Adam. The consequence of eating this forbidden fruit was death (2:17), and death would be known in two ways.

First, the violation of the command immediately polluted the Man and the Woman. Their damaged consciences exposed not only their physical state, but the two souls were weakened and a cold awareness swept over them (3:7). They had always sensed the warm, loving presence of God. Now the death chill of disobedience dominated the pair and God seemed very distant. They became, for the first time, fearful of contact with Him (3:10).

Second, covering their nakedness with fig leaves did not give any solace to their souls. Now they

understood that death's first manifestation was cata-
strophic spiritual separation from God. Now dread
overcame them, and in futility they tried to hide
themselves from His Omnipresence.

CONFRONTING AND EXPOSING
RELATIONAL FAILURE

The dialog between God and the fallen couple
reveals some interesting reactions (3:9-19). First,
God gave them an opportunity to acknowledge
responsibility, confess failure, and repent. All of this
is encapsulated in the Divine questions, "Where are
you?" and "What have you done?" Instead of accepting God's invitation, they both denied responsibility
and blamed someone else for their shame.

Second, their rebellion against the command of
God ravaged the tender relationship the Man and
the Woman had known. Now, instead of comple-
menting and caring for one another, selfishness sur-
faces as the ruling emotion. Adam implies that God
is responsible since He created the Woman and she
gave him the fruit to eat. One can only imagine the
sense of rejection she felt. The chasm is so deep
between them now that Adam distances himself further by giving the Woman another name—Eve
(3:20).

Third, God, who looks on the heart, says that
the Woman will have a different feeling for the
Man. It is called "desire" (3:16); however, stated in
the context of sin and judgment, it is not a warm
emotion. It is a sense of subjugation that will be
resisted and create an attitude of competition in her.
The risk of trusting herself to another is now a fear-

ful prospect. The relationship won't be the same.

Finally, God will not stand by passively at the marring of His premier creative act. In the midst of pronouncing judgment on the serpent, He states a coming reality that will provide the means of reconciliation between Him and people. Humans can have wholesome relationship with God once again based on the declaration that a divine Seed shall break the power of sin and death administered by the seed of the serpent (3:15).

REDEMPTIVE RELATIONAL COVENANTS

Thus begins a series of pronouncements by God called <u>covenants</u>. And it is these promises and their application that will provide restored relationship with God. They also offer the means of living with others in a manner that will be beneficial to all.

The grace and mercy of God is extended to all through these covenants. In Genesis, the guarantees were made by God with three men: Adam, Noah, and Abraham. Each covenant contains the redemptive promise. There are, however, distinctives in each covenant. The first offers the restoration of joy in relationships (3:15). The second underscores the fortifying of hope in relationships (9:9,11-13). And the third provides for the maintenance of faith in relationships (15:1,7,18; 17:1,2,4,5-7,10,11).

GOD'S COVENANT WITH
ADAM

And I will put enmity between you and the woman, and between your seed and her Seed; He shall bruise your head, and you shall bruise His heel (3:15).

THE WAY OF JOY—*Togetherness*

There was a time on earth when genuine joy filled the heart of Adam. This was true because of the fusion of his soul with the God through Whom creation was realized. Later, a comparable companion was created for him, and their shared life increased the joy for both. There are a number of things that will make a relationship joy-filled. Here are three:

    a.   Enjoying presence:
        Just being together is a cause for joy.
    b.   Enjoying fellowship:
        Doing things together brings joy.
    c.   Enjoying communication:
        Sharing thoughts and feelings increases joy.

THE DEATH OF JOY—*Disobedience*

Joy is a fragile commodity. It can be lost by a callous neglect for what is best for a relationship. In this case, a violation of God's counsel for what is best turned joy into dread.

    a.   Disregarding the commitment:
        The challenge of the third party.
    b.   Disobeying the command:
        Surrendering to temptation.

c. Destroying unity:
   Division is the consequence of relational failure.

THE LOSS OF JOY—*Selfishness*

When a relationship is rent, a survival mentality is engaged. The joy of sharing and serving is displaced by the desire for power and domination. All decisions are based on a "what's best for me" mentality. Thus selfishness becomes the bully that pummels the joy of relationship.

a. Denying responsibility:
   Blaming another for your failure.
b. Developing a protectionist attitude:
   Watching out for number one.

THE RECOVERY OF JOY—*Redemption*

The possibility of the return of joy is real. The surrender to sin and selfishness is dealt with in a redemptive promise. God who covered naked bodies will also make atonement for sin. The atonement He provides, through His grace and mercy, will lift guilt, reconcile the relationship, and restore joy.

a. The Promise of recovery:
   The redemption plan is put in motion.
b. The Procedure of recovery:
   A sacrifice will be the means of restoration.

GOD'S COVENANT WITH
NOAH

"Behold, I establish My covenant with you and with your descendants after you…Never again shall all flesh be cut off by waters of the flood; never again shall there be a flood to destroy the earth. And God said: 'This is the sign of the covenant which I make between Me and you, and every living creature that is with you, for perpetual generations: I set My rainbow in the cloud, and it shall be for the sign of the covenant between Me and the earth'" (9:9, 11-13).

HOPE WHEN THINGS GO BAD

Imagine living in a social environment where evil is the norm (6:11,12). The fabric of community is completely unraveled. As a matter of fact, in Noah's time, every conceivable act of wickedness was a regular occurrence. The actions of people expose the fact that they are driven by evil intents and thoughts continually (6:5). Things are so bad that God is grieved and sorry that He made people (6:6). Yet there is hope, for one man stands out and is the recipient of God's grace—one small light shining in the inky blackness of moral void. God's selection of Noah sends an eternal message of hope.

a. Grief over circumstances does not mean the defeat of hope.

b. God's judgment does not displace hope.

HOPE EMBRACED
BY ACTIONS

Being asked to do something that has never been done before can certainly challenge people. Despair can creep over those who believe what is being demanded is impossible because it has never been done before. It is important, however, to remember that when God gives the command and unveils His plan, nothing is impossible. When this reality is embraced, then actions demonstrate hope for the outcome.

a. Build something that witnesses to hope when surrounded by evil.

b. Bring others into the circle of hope.

c. Be secure in the atmosphere of hope.

HOPE WHEN ALL
IS LOST

Few things are more frightening than isolation. Natural disasters also are terrifying. This is what faced the small band in the Ark. The world they had known was gone. Except for the animals with them, all land life was lost. The questions that this condition raised must have been perplexing at best. What now? How can things begin anew? How long will it take? The issues of life can at times be overwhelming. Unless. Unless God is involved and it is His plan with which people are engaged.

a. Secure in God's command:
The will of God is paramount for people.

b. Secure in God's care:
There is safety in the place that God has led.

c. Secure in God's commitment:

Silence and time do not mean God has forgotten His people.

HOPE EXPRESSED
THROUGH WORSHIP

When people survive catastrophe they want to get at the job of cleaning up and getting their lives back together. But even after the situation is normalized there still is an unsettledness of soul. The reason is the fear of a recurring episode of disaster. It is expressed confidence in God that stabilizes hope. Worshipping God is the action that calms the soul, for no matter what lies ahead, His goodness and care provide the basis for hope in all things.

a.   Worship synthesizes God's grace (8:20).
b.   Worship secures the blessing of God (9:1).
c.   Worship seals the covenant with God (9:9,16).

GOD'S COVENANT WITH
ABRAHAM

"After these things the word of the LORD came to Abram in a vision, saying 'Do not be afraid, Abram. I am your shield, your exceedingly great reward' ... Then He said to him, 'I am the LORD, who brought you out of Ur of the Chaldeans, to give you this land to inherit it ...' On the same day the LORD made a covenant with Abram... When Abram was ninety-nine years old, the LORD appeared to Abram and said to him, 'I am Almighty God; walk before Me and be blameless, and

61

*I will make My covenant between Me and you, and
will multiply you exceedingly... My covenant is with
you, and you shall be a father of many nations. No
longer shall your name be called Abram, but your
name shall be Abraham; for I have made you a father
of many nations... And I will establish My covenant
between Me and you and your descendants after you in
their generations, for an everlasting covenant, to be
God to you and your descendants after you... As for
you, you shall keep My covenant, you and your descendants after you throughout their generations. This is
My covenant which you shall keep, between Me and
you and your descendants after you: Every male child
among you shall be circumcised; ...and it shall be a
sign of the covenant between Me and you'" (15:1,7,18;
17:1,2,4,5,10,11).*

FAITH'S FOCUS

Faith is not blind compliance to an unidentified
inner voice. It is not living by appeasing fate. Faith's
primeval expression is believing God exists and that
He can be known (Hebrews 11:6). On this basis
God reveals Himself and begins an interaction with
people that promises and produces blessing. The
focus of faith then is trust in God and acting on His
counsel.

    a.   Receiving God's promise (12:1-3).
    b.   Responding to God's promise (12:4; 13:3,4).
    c.   Rewarded through God's promise (15:6;
        18:10; 21:1-3).

FAITH'S FOOTING

Faith in God contains a dynamic element. It

grows and becomes stronger. It also can atrophy through neglect. Faith must be exercised in doing. The deeds of faith are based in the integrity of God's character and confidence in the continuity of His actions. He does not demand blind faith, but faith that is reasonable—reasonable because God is good, and because His goodness is demonstrable.

    a. Trust in God when asked to sacrifice what is loved most (22:1, 2).

    b. Trust prepares to do what is unthinkable (22:3, 7).

    c. Trust rests in the promises and provision of God (22:8).

    d. Trust is always rewarded (22:11-18).

FAITH'S FIGHT

God's promises will never fail. A promise given by the Lord is sure because He watches over it to bring it to completion (Romans 4:21). Yet people will be challenged to hold to these words of God. Patience is thin among most people, and human assistance does not hasten the fulfillment of God's word, it only creates tension and conflict. It is surrender to His way that procures faith's victory and keeps God's promise intact. Struggles with God and others intensify frustration and anger.

    a. Producing a son that is not the son (16:1-6,15,16; 17:18-21).

    b. Grasping the blessing instead of receiving the blessing (25:21-34; 27:1-42).

    c. Getting a wife that is not the wife (28:1,2; 29:1-28).

FAITH'S FUTURE

Faith for now is certainly important. Immediate concerns demand the most attention. While there is a high level of care given to present circumstances, faith secures the future, no matter what the present looks like. Applying faith on the contemporary scene will give temporary relief, but its fullest measure is best expressed in the promise of God which addresses the eternal realm. God's people must look beyond the temporal and let faith reveal the eternal.

 a. Believing in a dream requires faith (37:5-36; 45:1-8).
 b. Believing for justice requires faith (39:1-23).
 c. Believing for reconciliation requires faith (45:24-28; 46:29-31; 47:11,12).

RELATIONSHIPS
AND COVENANTS

Throughout the book of Genesis there are recorded interactions between God and people. The failure of people to respond to God has created many dilemmas for the human race. This is why people acted toward each other in controlling and manipulative ways. The moral and social whirlpool that resulted would have been devastating if God had not initiated redemptive actions. These acts by God were explained in His covenant relationships. They were not intended to deal only with a few folks in a crisis. It was God laying the groundwork for the time when, through His redeeming Agent, people would be reconciled in a loving, righteous, relationship with Him that makes possible the ability to live in unselfish, wholesome relationships with each other. Both the fulfillment of covenant promises and the word and ministry of reconciliation are made possible by Jesus Christ (2 Corinthians 1:20). And now, joy for living, hope in all things, and faith that rests, are the legacies for the descendants of Adam, Noah, and Abraham.

PRINCIPLES OF PURSUING THE WILL OF GOD

A Study in the Life of Abraham

Learn how to reach God's destiny for your life using the same principles Abraham followed.

In this 11-tape series on the life of Abraham, Pastor Jack Hayford presents practical principles which will equip and nurture a holy pursuit for the will of God in each believer's life. Your high destiny awaits, as you learn and practice these same principles.

Audio Album **PWG $45.00**

Want the Best Study Bible on the Market Today?

The

SPIRIT-FILLED LIFE BIBLE

may be what you're looking for!

The Spirit-Filled Life Bible is a powerful resource for enriching your relationship with Jesus Christ. Faith-filled, prophetic, and Spirit-empowered insights are featured in this one-of-a-kind study Bible. Here, in the light of God's Word, you will discover a Spirit-filled life rich in Godly characteristics.

This 2200-page, magnificently bound Bible is available from Living Way Ministries in either Burgundy or black genuine leather, and a classic hardback library edition—which is also available in English or Spanish.

Hardback Library Edition: *reg. $37.99* **SFLHB** **$27.99**
Burgundy Genuine Leather: *reg. $79.99* **SFLBG** **$54.99**
Black Genuine Leather: *reg. $79.99* **SGLBK** **$54.99**

A one-of-a-kind resource!

*Down-to-Earth Insight
for students of all ages!*

SPIRIT-FILLED LIFE BIBLE FOR STUDENTS

The Spirit-Filled Life Bible for students is a new dynamic tool that can help students deepen their spiritual roots and grow in Christ. This New King James Version resource for students offers real-life, down-to-earth insight for living the Christian life in today's world. General Editor Jack Hayford and nearly a dozen contributing authors have provided:

- Hundreds of helpful annotations.
- Maps and charts.
- Articles on major Bible themes.

This is a practical gift for students of any age who want to learn and live God's Word by the Power of His Spirit.

Softcover **SFLBS $15.99**

*This practical gift will help
your favorite student learn and live God's Word
by the Holy Spirit's power!*

Unveil the Keys to Scripture!

HAYFORD'S BIBLE HANDBOOK

Hayford's Bible Handbook is an unparalleled resource that uniquely unveils the keys to Scripture, providing not only a wealth of information, but also a spiritual stimulus that will encourage your faith and service to Christ.

It unlocks Scripture with:
- Illuminating surveys of each book of the Bible.
- Helpful illustrations, time lines, maps, and charts.
- A complete Visual Survey of the Bible.
- An Encyclopedia Dictionary with over 1,300 entries that address subjects of particular interest to Spirit-filled believers.

This guide opens the riches of Scripture with a unique focus on practical ministry in the Holy Spirit's power—all to deepen your life in Christ. *reg. $24.99* **HBH $22.99**

This guide will open the riches of Scripture and deepen your life in Christ!

ORDER FORM

Qty.	Item	Code	Price	Total

Postage and Handling

$0.00 - $9.99 . . . . $2.95
$10.00 - $29.99 . . . . $4.95
$30.00 - $59.99 . . . . $6.95
$60.00 and up . . . . . . Free (*In the U.S.*)
All orders outside the USA $8,
plus 20% of Subtotal

Subtotal _____

Add 8.25% sales tax to CA orders _____

Shipping and Handling _____

Donation (Optional) _____

Total _____

Name _____

Street Address _____

City _____ State _____ Zip _____

Phone Number (_____) _____

Method of Payment: ❑ Check or Money Order ❑ Visa ❑ MC

_____ / _____-_____-_____ / _____
Signature   Card Number   Exp. Date

RESOURCES

LIVING · WAY MINISTRIES

14820 Sherman Way, Van Nuys, CA 91405-2233

Please call for prices and ordering information:
1-800-776-8180 • 1-818-779-8480

Please include your remittance (U.S. currency only) with order.
Make check or money order payable to Living Way Ministries.